The

ULTIMATE TRAVEL JOURNAL

For Kids

United States of America

NEW HAMPSHIRE
MASSACHUSETTS
RHODE ISLAND
CONNECTICUT
NEW JERSEY
DELAWARE
MARYLAND
WASHINGTON, D.C.

MAINE
VERMONT
NEW YORK
PENNSYLVANIA
VIRGINIA
WEST VIRGINIA
NORTH CAROLINA
SOUTH CAROLINA
OHIO
GEORGIA
FLORIDA
MICHIGAN
INDIANA
KENTUCKY
TENNESSEE
ALABAMA
MISSISSIPPI
WISCONSIN
ILLINOIS
MISSOURI
ARKANSAS
LOUISIANA
IOWA
MINNESOTA
OKLAHOMA
KANSAS
NORTH DAKOTA
SOUTH DAKOTA
NEBRASKA
TEXAS
MONTANA
WYOMING
COLORADO
NEW MEXICO
UTAH
IDAHO
ARIZONA
NEVADA
WASHINGTON
OREGON
CALIFORNIA

ALASKA
HAWAII

The ULTIMATE
TRAVEL
JOURNAL
for Kids

INCLUDES **4** TRIPS!

**ROCKRIDGE
PRESS**

Cover and Interior Designer: Merideth Harte
Art Manager: Sue Bischofberger
Editor: Salwa Jabado
Production Editor: Erum Khan
Illustrations by Steve Mack
Author photo courtesy of Chris Taylor

ISBN: Print 978-1-64152-421-6

This JOURNAL belongs to:

Age:

TRIP № 1

GREENLAND

U.S.A.
ALASKA

CANADA

ICELAND

UNITED STATES OF AMERICA

BERMUDA (U.K.)

U.S.A.
HAWAII

TURKS & CAICOS ISLANDS (U.K.)
DOMINICAN REPUBLIC
PUERTO RICO (U.S.A.)
U.S. VIRGIN ISLANDS
BRITISH VIRGIN ISLANDS
ANGUILLA
ST. MARTIN
ST. BARTHÉLEMY
ST. KITTS & NEVIS
ANTIGUA & BARBUDA
DOMINICA
MARTINIQUE
BARBADOS
TRINIDAD & TOBAGO

MEXICO

CUBA

BAHAMAS

HAITI

BELIZE
JAMAICA

GUATEMALA
EL SALVADOR
HONDURAS
COSTA RICA

NICARAGUA

PANAMA

GUADELOUPE
ST. LUCIA

VENEZUELA

COLOMBIA

GUYANA

SURINAME

FRENCH GUIANA

ECUADOR

PERU

BRAZIL

BOLIVIA

PARAGUAY

CHILE

ARGENTINA

URUGUAY

FALKLAND ISLANDS (ISLAS MALVINAS) (U.K.)

1

 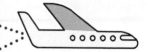

Where I'm headed...

It's time to hit the road! I'm on my way to

from   . I'm packing some important

stuff, like   and   .

I'm leaving on *(date)*   and

should return home on *(date)*   ,

unless I love it so much that I just have to stay

forever . . .

The people I'm traveling with are

.

I feel   about this trip.

The best part of traveling:

DISCOVERY

Destination:

Expected climate / weather:

This place is known for   ,

                        , and   .

I'm most excited to   .

This is what I hope will happen:

                                                           .

I predict that I'm going to see some strange or

different people or foods. Here are some things I'm

not so sure about:

ALONG THE WAY, I'VE FOUND...

They say that half the fun of travel is the journey to the destination... *(circle one)* **I AGREE** or **I DISAGREE.**

Our trip started by *(circle one)*:

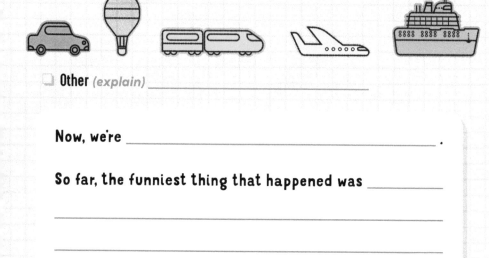

❏ **Other** *(explain)* _____

Now, we're _____ .

So far, the funniest thing that happened was _____

_____

_____

_____ .

I had no idea that _____

_____

_____

_____ .

KEEP YOUR EYES PEELED!

Can you find all the items on the board below?
Watch out for each of these items throughout your trip,
and if you see one, X it out. Fill in all the spaces for a
total blackout, or go in a line across, up and down, or
diagonally from corner to corner for Bingo!

BOREDOM
BANISHER!

Windmill	sign in another language	Public art	Solar panel	Large mammal
Fountain	Train	Neon sign	Non-airplane flying object	Danger sign
Person on horse	Chickens	Map	Tourists taking photos	Dog walker
Large mural	Someone writing	Tunnel	Frog	Building taller than 10 stories
Taxi	Person in a uniform	Souvenir	Gargoyle	Pink vehicle

Hint: Ask an adult if you can make a deal with them to score an
awesome prize for completing the blackout board.

HERE'S HOW IT'S GOING ON THIS TRIP...

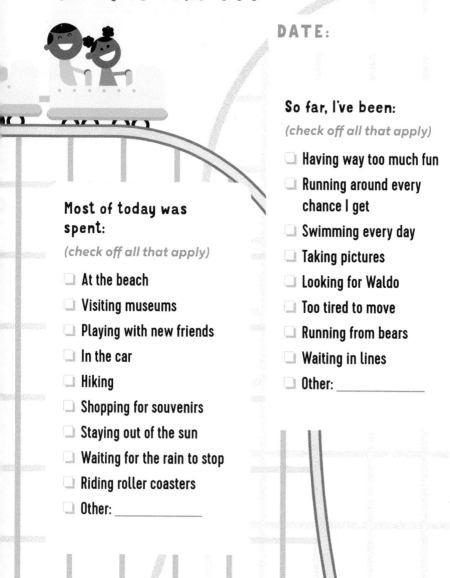

DATE:

So far, I've been:

(check off all that apply)

- ☐ Having way too much fun
- ☐ Running around every chance I get
- ☐ Swimming every day
- ☐ Taking pictures
- ☐ Looking for Waldo
- ☐ Too tired to move
- ☐ Running from bears
- ☐ Waiting in lines
- ☐ Other: _____

Most of today was spent:

(check off all that apply)

- ☐ At the beach
- ☐ Visiting museums
- ☐ Playing with new friends
- ☐ In the car
- ☐ Hiking
- ☐ Shopping for souvenirs
- ☐ Staying out of the sun
- ☐ Waiting for the rain to stop
- ☐ Riding roller coasters
- ☐ Other: _____

TRYING NEW FOOD

Normally I like to eat _____,

but I just tried eating _____ at

(name of place) _____,

and *(circle one)* **I LOVED IT / LIKED IT / WAS GROSSED OUT BY IT.**

I felt this way because _____

_____.

Draw a picture of what the food looked like.

THE PEOPLE I MET

Airplane pilots, tour guides, and restaurant servers, oh my! You always meet so many new people on a trip. To make sure I remember them, I've decided to get their autographs!

(Let people sign below.)

The person I'll remember most is   ,

because

NEW EXPERIENCES ON THE ROAD ⇨ → DATE:

Today, the weather was *(circle one)*:

   ☐ Other_____

 An awesome new experience I had was

 The part that wasn't so great was

 When I get home, I'm going to tell everyone about

(Draw in the needle to show how awesome your day was.)

ALMOST HOME!

DATE:

Wow! I can't believe this trip is almost over. I've done and seen so much!

The most exciting thing I did was

.

The most beautiful sight I saw was

.

My most grown-up moment was

.

I learned so much. I now know

.

10

THE ___(fill in the blank)___ DAY EVER!

Fill in the blanks to write a story about your day. Ask your fellow travelers to fill in the blank parts of speech, but don't read or show them the story until it's done.

Wow! Today was seriously the *(superlative [-est])* _____

day ever. When I woke up, I knew we were going to

(verb) _____ a *(noun)* _____ ,

but I had no idea it would be so *(adjective)* _____!

First, we had *(adjective)* _____

(food) _____ for breakfast and then,

right after that, we *(past verb)* _____ at the

(place) _____. It's been nonstop and now I desperately

need a *(noun)* _____. I thought we

were going to *(verb)* _____ before seeing

the *(noun)* _____, but we ended up

(active verb [-ing]) _____ the *(noun)* _____

instead. I really liked when we *(past verb)* _____

at the *(place)* _____. I saw so many

(plural noun) _____—at least *(number)* ___!

What a day. *(Superlative [-est])* _____

day ever!

SHADE-IN SURPRISE!

Fill in the squares that coordinate with each letter and number listed to the right to reveal a hidden image.

	1	2	3	4	5	6	7	8	9	10	11	12	13	14	15	16	17	18	19	20	21	22
V																						
U																						
T																						
S																						
R																						
Q																						
P																						
O																						
N																						
M																						
L																						
K																						
J																						
I																						
H																						
G																						
F																						
E																						
D																						
C																						
B																						
A																						
0	1	2	3	4	5	6	7	8	9	10	11	12	13	14	15	16	17	18	19	20	21	22

M12	B8	B19	I2	A8
E17	K6	J3	K14	T4
A19	J5	H16	J2	L5
C17	J14	C8	U5	B10
E14	A20	M16	K15	H5
H4	U3	B21	M13	J12
A21	P14	L2	P3	H11
I12	J15	E13	D13	L3
F12	K1	I13	P5	R14
M15	J7	R4	I6	L6
I5	G12	K12	O13	J16
C9	P4	J13	I4	C19
I11	A6	U4	E12	G4
G17	U14	N15	D19	C11
O15	C10	I17	L14	K4
P15	H12	G11	J6	A22
K7	S14	D15	D12	P13
G16	I15	A7	F17	D16
K2	Q14	E11	L16	D18
Q4	E15	B18	B9	A9
I16	H17	K3	J1	H3
D17	C18	K5	D14	N13
D10	D11	L13	O14	D9
B20	V14	E16	B7	E18
T14	I3	E10	C20	
K16	J4	L12	K13	
F11	L15	S4	F16	

See page 76 for the answer!

EXPRESS yourself

Use these pages to draw, freewrite, or tape selfies, tickets, or other paper souvenirs from your trip.

In **CONNECTICUT**, it is illegal to sell a pickle that does not bounce when dropped from a one-foot height.

Use these pages to freewrite.

DUDE, THAT IS WEIRD!

The weirdest thing I have seen so far was _____
_____
_____ .

It was weird because _____
_____
_____ .

I know that my life and where I live is way different from the place I'm visiting. Is this "weird" thing strange to the people who live here OR is it weird to me because it's so different from what I see at home? _____
_____
_____ .

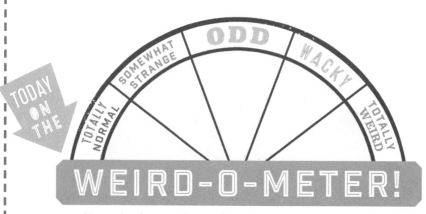

(Draw in the needle to show how weird your day was.)

TOP 5

NEW OR COOL THINGS
I SAW ON THIS TRIP

19

TRIP № 2

GREENLAND

ICELAND

U.S.A.
ALASKA

CANADA

UNITED STATES OF AMERICA

U.S.A.
HAWAII

BERMUDA (U.K.)
TURKS & CAICOS ISLANDS (U.K.)
DOMINICAN REPUBLIC
PUERTO RICO (U.S.A.)
U.S. VIRGIN ISLANDS
BRITISH VIRGIN ISLANDS
ANGUILLA
ST. MARTIN
ST. BARTHÉLEMY
ST. KITTS & NEVIS
ANTIGUA & BARBUDA
DOMINICA
MARTINIQUE
BARBADOS
TRINIDAD & TOBAGO

MEXICO
CUBA
HAITI
BELIZE
JAMAICA
GUATEMALA
NICARAGUA
EL SALVADOR
HONDURAS
PANAMA
COSTA RICA

BAHAMAS

GUADELOUPE
ST. LUCIA

VENEZUELA
COLOMBIA
GUYANA
SURINAME
FRENCH GUIANA

ECUADOR
PERU
BRAZIL
BOLIVIA
PARAGUAY

CHILE
ARGENTINA
URUGUAY

FALKLAND ISLANDS (ISLAS MALVINAS) (U.K.)

2·1

Where I'm headed...

It's time to hit the road! I'm on my way to _____

_____ from _____ . I've packed

these things that I don't think I can live without:

_____ . I wish I could

pack _____

_____ !

I'm leaving on (date) _____

and should return home on (date) _____ ,

unless I love it so much that I just have to stay

forever . . .

The people I'm traveling with are _____

_____

_____ .

I feel _____ about this trip!

The best part of traveling:

Learning
Something New!

Destination:

Have you been here before? *(circle one)* **Yes / No**

If yes, what are some things you remember about this

place: _____ , _____ ,

and _____ .

Expected climate / weather: _____

This place is known for _____ .

_____ , and _____ .

I heard that I have to try *(activity or food)* _____

_____ . This is what I think I'll love

about it: _____

_____

_____

DATE:

I THOUGHT I WAS READY FOR THIS TRIP, AND BOY WAS I... *(check one)*

☐ SURPRISED ☐ ABSOLUTELY READY ☐ TOTALLY UNPREPARED

To prepare for visiting _____ , I made sure to

_____

_____ .

I'm ready for anything. Did you know that I'm even

prepared for _____

_____ ?

You know, just in case _____

_____ .

And good thing, too. I had no idea that _____

_____

_____ .

DID YOU KNOW?

The national animal of SCOTLAND is the ...
unicorn!

BEST SOUVENIR EVER!

There's more to life than stuff, but finding a special souvenir is great because _____

_____.

I'm *(circle one)* **looking for / I've found** _____

_____.

I think this is a special souvenir because _____

_____.

(Draw a picture of your special souvenir or what you're looking for.)

VACATION WILL BE RELAXING, THEY SAID . . .

So far, we've done all of these things:
(check off all that apply)

- ☐ Swam
- ☐ Visited a museum
- ☐ Had 100 bathroom breaks
- ☐ Endlessly looked for parking
- ☐ Ate outside
- ☐ Used an umbrella
- ☐ Hiked
- ☐ Bundled up

- ☐ Stayed out of the sun
- ☐ Took at least three group pictures
- ☐ Met somebody important (or famous)
- ☐ Went souvenir shopping
- ☐ Saw wildlife
- ☐ Other: _____

My favorite activity so far has been _____

_____

_____ .

The reason I enjoyed this so much is because _____

_____

_____

_____

_____ .

NEW EXPERIENCES ON THE ROAD ⇒ → DATE:

Today, **the weather was** *(circle one)*:

  ☐ Other

 #1 An awesome new experience I had was

 The part that wasn't so great was

When I get home, I'm going to tell everyone about

(Draw in the needle to show how awesome your day was.)

EXPRESS yourself

Use these pages to draw, freewrite, or tape selfies, tickets, or other paper souvenirs from your trip.

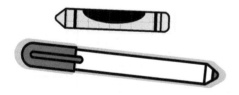

You can spend real coins with Mickey Mouse's picture on them in a small South Pacific country called NIUE.

EXPRESS yourself

Use these pages to freewrite.

AROUND THE WORLD CROSSWORD PUZZLE

ACROSS

2. Mushy, snap, or green _____
3. Today's name for Bombay
6. Best for flying
9. River with pink dolphins
10. Floating hotel
11. Continent with penguins
14. 50th U.S. state
15. Rides the rails

DOWN

1. National animal of Australia
4. Tool for watching faraway wildlife
5. Buttery, flaky French pastry
7. ____ 66
8. Takes pics
10. Sleeping in a tent
12. Home of lasagna and the Leaning Tower of Pisa
13. Great Wall of _____

PACKING LIST WORD SCRAMBLE

Unscramble the words to reveal your packing list.

1. sohbhottur
2. htoeaotpts
3. aecmra
4. boko
5. ltaver luarojn
6. lpfi opsfl
7. simwsitu
8. glegsog
9. esgsuslsna
10. psen
11. liepcns
12. rduawrnee
13. jaamsap
14. shrtso
15. trissh
16. ehsos
17. tha
18. tspna
19. cossk
20. aetcjk
21. uelrmalb

See page 77 for the crossword and word scramble answers.

MY DAY AWAY!

I woke up at

.

The first thing I did was

.

We headed out for the day to

.

One interesting thing I saw or did this morning:

.

For lunch I had

.

This afternoon we

.

Today was

because

.

TOP 5 FAVORITE PLACES I VISITED

TRIP № 3

GREENLAND

U.S.A.
ALASKA

CANADA

ICELAND

UNITED STATES OF AMERICA

U.S.A.
HAWAII

BERMUDA (U.K.)
TURKS & CAICOS ISLANDS (U.K.)
DOMINICAN REPUBLIC
PUERTO RICO (U.S.A.)
BAHAMAS
U.S. VIRGIN ISLANDS
BRITISH VIRGIN ISLANDS
ANGUILLA
ST. MARTIN
ST. BARTHÉLEMY
ST. KITTS & NEVIS
ANTIGUA & BARBUDA
DOMINICA
GUADELOUPE
ST. LUCIA
MARTINIQUE
BARBADOS
TRINIDAD & TOBAGO

MEXICO
CUBA
BELIZE
HAITI
JAMAICA
GUATEMALA
EL SALVADOR
NICARAGUA
HONDURAS
PANAMA
COSTA RICA

VENEZUELA
GUYANA
SURINAME
COLOMBIA
FRENCH GUIANA

ECUADOR
PERU

BRAZIL

BOLIVIA
PARAGUAY

ARGENTINA
URUGUAY

CHILE

FALKLAND ISLANDS (ISLAS MALVINAS) (U.K.)

37

WHERE I'M HEADED

It's time to hit the road! I'm on my way to _____

from _____ . I'm packing some important

stuff, like _____ and _____ .

I'm leaving on *(date)* _____ and

should return home on *(date)* _____ ,

unless I love it so much that I just have to stay

forever...

The people I'm traveling with are _____

_____

_____

_____ .

I feel _____

_____

_____ about this trip.

The best part of traveling:

DISCOVERY

Destination: _____

Expected climate / weather: _____

This place is known for _____ ,

_____ , and _____ .

I'm most excited to _____ .

This is what I hope will happen: _____

_____

_____ .

I predict that I'm going to see some strange or different

people or foods. Here are some things I'm not so sure

about: _____

_____

_____

_____ .

ALONG THE WAY, I'VE FOUND...

They say that half the fun of travel is the journey to the destination . . . *(circle one)* **I AGREE** or **I DISAGRE**.

Our trip started by *(circle one)*:

❏ **Other** *(explain)*_____

Now, we're _____ .

So far, the funniest thing that happened was _____

_____

_____ .

I had no idea that _____

_____

_____ .

DID YOU KNOW?

In CALIFORNIA, it's illegal to eat a frog that dies in a frog-jumping contest.

HERE'S WHAT I'M THINKING ABOUT THIS TRIP . . .

Most of today was spent:
(check off all that apply)

- ☐ At the beach
- ☐ Visiting museums
- ☐ Playing with new friends
- ☐ In the car
- ☐ Shopping for souvenirs
- ☐ Hiking
- ☐ Staying out of the sun
- ☐ Waiting for the rain to stop
- ☐ Riding roller coasters
- ☐ Other _____

So far, I've been:
(check off all that apply)

- ☐ Having way too much fun
- ☐ Running around every chance I get
- ☐ Swimming every day
- ☐ Taking pictures
- ☐ Looking for Waldo
- ☐ Too tired to move
- ☐ Running from bears
- ☐ Waiting in lines
- ☐ Other _____

MUSEUM

MARCO POLO'S JOURNEY

One of the most famous travelers of all time was Marco Polo. He was born on the island of Korčula in modern-day Croatia ... or he was from the city of Venice—it's actually a mystery! He ended his lifelong journey around Europe and Asia back in Venice.

Help Marco navigate the seas from Asia and everywhere else back to Venice.

MY DAYDREAM

I think what this trip needs is

_____

_____

_____

_____ .

Just think, if we could _____

_____

_____ , then _____

_____

_____

_____

_____ .

NEW PLACES WORD SEARCH

Find the words at the bottom of the page in the word search, and circle your answers. Search up, down, and diagonally to find the hidden words.

```
H   N   E   R   U   S   S   I   A   J   S   A   F   K   P
N   E   O   W   V   B   K   Q   C   O   Q   N   K   E   R
F   T   N   R   U   E   N   O   X   A   K   T   W   H   F
N   U   A   S   T   X   W   K   C   M   U   A   X   S   K
M   V   U   O   V   H   X   I   F   O   C   R   E   X   Y
G   A   S   U   N   A   A   P   T   K   F   C   U   L   M
O   T   T   T   C   D   F   M   R   S   I   T   R   D   C
N   I   R   H   T   S   B   R   E   M   T   I   O   P   H
L   C   A   A   W   X   C   F   I   R   P   C   P   V   I
C   A   L   M   A   R   X   Q   X   C   I   A   E   M   N
F   N   I   E   S   V   U   S   U   J   A   C   Y   C   A
I   C   A   R   I   X   U   G   E   Z   X   D   A   G   P
C   I   B   I   A   N   X   S   H   A   N   G   H   A   I
H   T   D   C   F   Y   B   Q   T   U   P   N   Y   C   Q
K   Y   G   A   V   X   A   C   N   N   Q   K   N   N   Y
```

The 7 continents:
Africa
Europe
Asia
North America
South America
Australia
Antarctica

Biggest country by land mass: Russia

Smallest country by land mass: Vatican City

Biggest country by people: China

Biggest city by people: Shanghai

See page 77 for the answer!

44

MY DAY

DATE: _____

I woke up at _____.

The first thing I did was _____.

We headed out for the day to _____.

One interesting thing I saw or did this morning: _____

_____

_____

_____.

For lunch I had _____.

This afternoon we _____

_____

_____.

The funniest thing that happened today was _____

_____

_____

_____.

TAXI

TAXI

OUTSIDE MY WINDOW

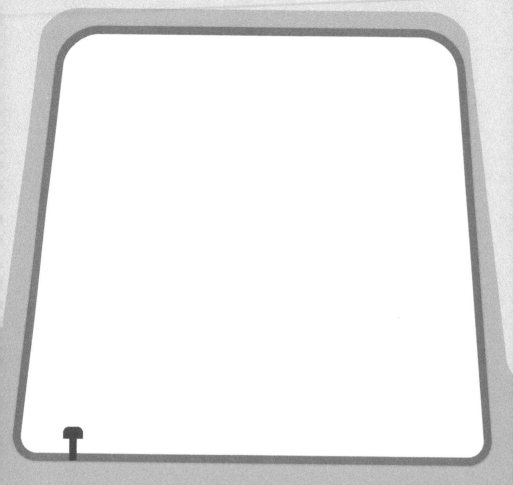

Draw what you can see outside
your window right now.

DATE:

NEW EXPERIENCES ON THE ROAD ⇨ ➡ DATE:

Today, the weather was *(circle one)*:

    ☐ Other

 An awesome new experience I had was

.

 The part that wasn't so great was

.

When I get home, I'm going to tell everyone about

.

TODAY ON THE

BLAH OKAY PRETTY GOOD AWESOME BEST DAY EVER

AWESOME-O-METER!

(Draw in the needle to show how awesome your day was.)

ALMOST HOME!

DATE:

Wow! I can't believe this trip is almost over. I've done and seen so much!

The most exciting thing I did was

.

The most beautiful sight I saw was

.

My most grown-up moment was

.

I learned so much. I now know

.

CAR GAMES FOR THE LONG RIDE HOME #1

I'm Going to _____, and I'm Bringing _____: Memory Game

This memory game is played with two or more players. Customize this game with your destination and then name the goofy things you might be bringing with you. The first player starts by naming something they will bring that starts with the letter A, and the next player has to repeat what the first player is bringing and then add to it with a word that starts with the next letter of the alphabet. For example:

The first player says: I'm going to Disney World and I'm bringing an autograph book.

The next player says: I'm going to Disney World and I'm bringing an autograph book and a beach ball.

The game continues until a player can no longer remember everything you're bringing—or you finish the alphabet!

The Principal's Cat: Quick-Thinking Game

This game is played with two or more players—the more players, the better. Everyone claps their hands slowly and steadily. In time with the rhythm, the first player chants a describing word about the principal's cat. Then, without missing a beat, the next player chants something different about the principal's cat. For example:

Clap-clap-clap-clap

The principal's cat is a black cat.

The principal's cat is a sleeping cat.

The principal's cat is a happy cat.

The game continues until the rhythm is broken or a nonsense word is used! If you want an even bigger challenge, go in alphabetical order.

EXPRESS yourself

Use these pages to draw, freewrite, or tape selfies, tickets, or other paper souvenirs from your trip.

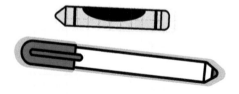

The GREAT WALL OF CHINA is estimated at 5,500 feet long. That's longer than the distance from Miami, Florida to Anchorage, Alaska!

LIFE IS FULL OF "FIRSTS"

Travel is all about new experiences. Think about yesterday and today . . .

For the first time ever, I

Would I do it again? *(circle one)* **YES / NO** Why?:

I learned that I can

I think this is important because

TOP 5 THINGS TO WRITE HOME ABOUT

Write them in the postcards. Make sure you include the person's name who you are writing to!

Dear

Dear

Dear

Dear

Dear

55

TRIP № 4

GREENLAND

U.S.A.
ALASKA

CANADA

ICELAND

U.S.A.
HAWAII

UNITED STATES OF AMERICA

BERMUDA (U.K.)
TURKS & CAICOS ISLANDS (U.K.)
DOMINICAN REPUBLIC
PUERTO RICO (U.S.A.)
U.S. VIRGIN ISLANDS
BRITISH VIRGIN ISLANDS
ANGUILLA
ST. MARTIN
ST. BARTHÉLEMY
ST. KITTS & NEVIS
ANTIGUA & BARBUDA
DOMINICA
MARTINIQUE
BARBADOS
TRINIDAD & TOBAGO

BAHAMAS

MEXICO   CUBA
                    HAITI
           BELIZE
           JAMAICA
GUATEMALA   NICARAGUA   GUADELOUPE
EL SALVADOR   ST. LUCIA
HONDURAS
COSTA RICA   PANAMA
                         VENEZUELA   GUYANA
                    COLOMBIA   SURINAME
                                                    FRENCH GUIANA
ECUADOR

            PERU
                         BRAZIL

            BOLIVIA
                    PARAGUAY

                              URUGUAY

CHILE   ARGENTINA

FALKLAND ISLANDS (ISLAS MALVINAS) (U.K.)

56

57

Where I'm Headed...

I'm off on another adventure, and it's time to hit the road!

I'm on my way to _____

from _____ .

I've packed _____

_____ because now that I'm a real

traveler, I know I need it!

I'm leaving on *(date)* _____

and should return home on *(date)* _____ ,

unless I love it so much that I just have to stay

forever...

The people I'm traveling with are _____

_____

_____ .

The best part of traveling:

LEARNING SOMETHING NEW

Destination: ____

Have you been here before? *(circle one)* Yes / No

If yes, what are some things you remember? __________

________________________________, ________________

____________________, and ___________________________.

Expected climate / weather: __________________________

This place is known for ______________________________,

_________________________, and ______________________.

I heard that I have to try *(activity or food)* __________

____.

This is what I think I'll love about it: ______________

____

____

ALONG THE WAY, I'VE FOUND...

They say that half the fun of travel is the journey to the destination... *(circle one)* **I AGREE** or **I DISAGREE**.

Our trip started by *(circle one)*:

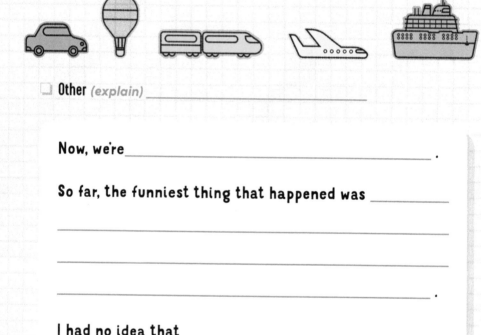

☐ **Other** *(explain)* _____

Now, we're _____ .

So far, the funniest thing that happened was _____

_____

_____

_____ .

I had no idea that _____

_____

_____ .

CONNECT THE DOTS

Connect the dots from 1 to 26.

Now, draw something interesting you saw today in the frame above.

Location and date: _____

VACATION WILL BE RELAXING, THEY SAID...

So far we've done all of these things:
(check off all that apply)

- ☐ Slept in a tent
- ☐ Swam
- ☐ Visited a museum
- ☐ Had 100 bathroom breaks
- ☐ Endlessly looked for parking
- ☐ Hiked
- ☐ Ate outside

- ☐ Used an umbrella
- ☐ Stayed out of the sun
- ☐ Took at least three group pictures
- ☐ Met somebody important (or famous)
- ☐ Went souvenir shopping
- ☐ Saw wildlife

My favorite activity so far has been _____

_____ .

The reason I enjoyed this so much is because _____

_____

_____

_____

_____

_____ .

NEW EXPERIENCES
ON THE ROAD ⇒ → DATE:

Today, the weather was *(circle one)*:

   ☐ Other

 An awesome new experience I had was

 The part that wasn't so great was

When I get home, I'm going to tell everyone about

TODAY ON THE — AWESOME-O-METER!

BLAH · OKAY · PRETTY GOOD · AWESOME · BEST DAY EVER

(Draw in the needle to show how awesome your day was.)

WHAT. DID. I. JUST. SEE?!

Fill in the blanks to write a story about your day. Ask your fellow travelers to fill in the blank parts of speech, but don't read or show them the story until it's done.

You won't even believe what I just saw! A (animal) _____

(past verb) _____ past me. You know, I heard that

it was normal to see a (animal) _____ here, but

I had no idea it would be so (adjective) _____ .

It must have been (number) _____ feet tall and was as fast

as a (noun) _____ ! I think that's what's so

(adjective) _____ about traveling:

You never expect (adjective) _____ (plural noun) _____

_____ to (verb) _____ . When I get home,

I'm going to tell (friend's name) _____

all about this. They won't even believe me. I mean,

(noun) _____ sightings are so rare they're

going to think I'm (adjective) _____ . That's

okay, though. I know what happened and I'm so glad I got to

(verb) _____ . What an experience!

(superlative [-est]) _____ story ever.

I THOUGHT I WAS READY FOR THIS TRIP, AND BOY WAS I . . . (check one)

❑ SURPRISED   ❑ ABSOLUTELY READY   ❑ TOTALLY UNPREPARED

To prepare for visiting _____ , I made sure to

_____ .

I'm ready for anything. Did you know that I'm even prepared for

_____ ?

You know, just in case

_____ .

And good thing, too. I had no idea that

_____ .

JUST FOR FUN:

Are you in a public place? Look around and see who looks the most like a famous person or someone you know. What do your fellow travelers think?

TRYING NEW FOOD

DATE:

Normally I like to eat _____ ,

but I just tried eating _____ at

(name of place) _____ ,

and *(circle one)* **I LOVED IT / LIKED IT / WAS GROSSED OUT BY IT.**

I felt this way because _____

_____ .

Draw a picture of what the food looked like.

LIST IT!

See how many items you can list in each category. If more than one person will play the game, make it a competition! See how many words you can come up with in one minute, then compare and see who got the most!

Countries

Sports

Breeds of Dogs

Ice Cream Flavors

EXPRESS yourself

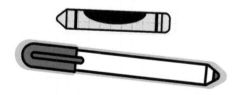

Use these pages to draw, freewrite, or tape selfies, tickets, or other paper souvenirs from your trip.

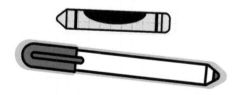

In MISSOURI, it is illegal to drive with an uncaged bear.

Use these pages to freewrite.

CAR GAMES FOR THE LONG RIDE HOME #2

First Letter, Last Letter: Travel Edition

This game needs two or more players. The first person says the name of a place, like Montreal. The next person has to name a place that starts with the last letter in Montreal. They choose Louisiana. The next person has to come up with a place that starts with the last letter in Louisiana, and so on.

You can change up the categories, too. For example: foods, items in a suitcase, animals, countries, and so on.

Fortunately, Unfortunately: Storytelling Game

This storytelling game can go as far as your imagination takes you. You'll need two or more players. The first player begins the story by introducing a character.

Xavier got into his car with his family and headed north.

The second player then describes a fortunate (good) stroke of luck the character has had. For example:

Fortunately, he is going on vacation to Maine.

The next player (or the first player if there are only two) keeps the story going with an unfortunate turn of bad luck. For example:

Unfortunately, a giant moose has been spotted in the hotel where he will be staying.

Then the next player adds to the story with *Fortunately* again:

Fortunately, someone has tamed the moose and is now offering moose rides for $1.

Unfortunately, ...

The game ends when everyone is laughing because the story is too ridiculous to go on, or when you want a new story or character.

TOP 5

FAVORITE ACTIVITIES I'VE DONE ON THIS TRIP

Can you find and circle the: unicorn, LOVE miniature highland cow, tent, truck with camper, horse with rider, pagoda, gondola with gondolier, sunglasses emoji and windmill?

74

Acknowledgments

This project was made possible thanks to the two little people that inspire me to keep exploring and sharing the world with them.

About the Author

ROB TAYLOR is a travel writer from the Pacific Northwest, a photographer, and most importantly, a dad. Focusing on family travel and education in the outdoors, Rob has spent years creating travel itineraries and guides to help families experience cities, nature, and small towns around the world. Rob's collective works, which focus on education as part of travel, are available through 2TravelDads.com and a variety of print publications.

Answer Key

Below, you'll find the answers to the Shade in Surprise! (page 12), Around the World Crossword Puzzle (page 32), Packing List Word Scramble (page 33), and New Places Word Search (page 44).

SHADE-IN SURPRISE:

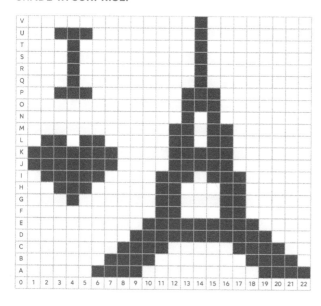

AROUND THE WORLD CROSSWORD PUZZLE:

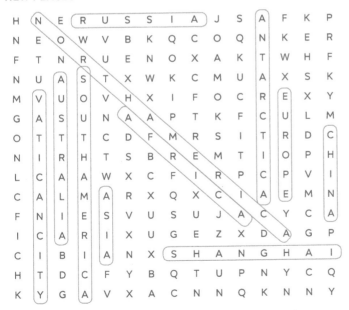

PACKING LIST WORD SCRAMBLE: toothbrush, toothpaste, camera, book, travel journal, flip flops, swimsuit, goggles, sunglasses, pens, pencils, underwear, pajamas, shorts, shirts, shoes, hat, pants, socks, jacket, umbrella

NEW PLACES WORD SEARCH:

H	N	E	R	U	S	S	I	A	J	S	A	F	K	P
N	E	O	W	V	B	K	Q	C	O	Q	N	K	E	R
F	T	N	R	U	E	N	O	X	A	K	T	W	H	F
N	U	A	S	T	X	W	K	C	M	U	A	X	S	K
M	V	U	O	V	H	X	I	F	O	C	R	E	X	Y
G	A	S	U	N	A	A	P	T	K	F	C	U	L	M
O	T	T	T	C	D	F	M	R	S	I	T	R	D	C
N	I	R	H	T	S	B	R	E	M	T	I	O	P	H
L	C	A	A	W	X	C	F	I	R	P	C	P	V	I
C	A	L	M	A	R	X	Q	X	C	I	A	E	M	N
F	N	I	E	S	V	U	S	U	J	A	C	Y	C	A
I	C	A	R	I	X	U	G	E	Z	X	D	A	G	P
C	I	B	I	A	N	X	S	H	A	N	G	H	A	I
H	T	D	C	F	Y	B	Q	T	U	P	N	Y	C	Q
K	Y	G	A	V	X	A	C	N	N	Q	K	N	N	Y

CPSIA information can be obtained
at www.ICGtesting.com
Printed in the USA
BVHW060810130719
553172BV00004BA/5/P